First World War
and Army of Occupation
War Diary
France, Belgium and Germany

2 DIVISION
3 Light Brigade
Rifle Brigade (The Prince Consort's Own)
52 Battalion
1 March 1919 - 21 October 1919

WO95/1374/11

The Naval & Military Press Ltd
www.nmarchive.com
Published in association with The National Archives

Published by

The Naval & Military Press Ltd

Unit 10 Ridgewood Industrial Park,

Uckfield, East Sussex,

TN22 5QE England

Tel: +44 (0) 1825 749494

www.naval-military-press.com

www.nmarchive.com

This diary has been reprinted in facsimile from the original. Any imperfections are inevitably reproduced and the quality may fall short of modern type and cartographic standards.

© **Crown Copyright**
Images reproduced by permission of The National Archives, London, England, 2015.

Contents

Document type	Place/Title	Date From	Date To
Heading	WO95/1374/11		
Heading	2 Division 3 Light Brigade 52 Bn The Rifle Bde 1919 Mar-1919 Oct		
War Diary	Dunkerque	01/03/1919	01/03/1919
War Diary	In The Train	02/03/1919	03/03/1919
War Diary	Germany	04/03/1919	31/03/1919
War Diary	Worringen	01/04/1919	07/04/1919
War Diary	Konigshoven	08/04/1919	30/04/1919
War Diary	Worringen	01/04/1919	07/04/1919
War Diary	Konigshoven	08/04/1919	17/06/1919
War Diary	Line Of March	18/06/1919	19/06/1919
War Diary	Mungersdorf	20/06/1919	20/06/1919
War Diary	Line Of March Suly Cologne	21/06/1919	26/06/1919
War Diary	Sulz-Cologne	27/06/1919	30/06/1919
War Diary	Konigshoven	01/07/1919	08/07/1919
War Diary	Hilden	09/07/1919	31/08/1919
War Diary	Germany Hilden	01/09/1919	30/09/1919
War Diary	Hilden	01/10/1919	21/10/1919

WO 95/1374/11

~~LIGHT~~ 2 (2) DIVISION

3 LIGHT BRIGADE

5/2 BN THE RIFLE BDE

1919 MAR – 1919 OCT

5nd Batt. The Rifle Brigade.

WAR DIARY
or
INTELLIGENCE SUMMARY.

Army Form C. 2118.

Place	Date	Hour	Summary of Events and Information	Remarks and references to Appendices
Dunkerque.	March 1st	08.00	The Bn entrained at Sandag sidings for Germany. Owing to a shortage of engines the troop train was delayed for some hours, eventually leaving Dunkerque at 16.00 hours.	
In the train.	2nd	05.00	The train reached MERRIS, where a halt was made for breakfast which was served in a dot camp. BAISIEUX the next halting place was reached at 16.00 hours.	
do.	3rd		CHARLEROI was reached in the early hours of the morning & a halt was made for breakfast. Thence through HUY & LIEGE the journey was continued, the train finally crossing into German territory at 22.15 hours.	
Germany.	4th		The troop train, having passed through COLOGNE in the early hours of the morning arrived at WORRINGEN, its destination at 04.00 hours. The Battn detrained and marched to billets. Hqrs. & 1 Coy at LANGEL. 2 Coy at FUHLINGEN. & 1 Coy at RHEINKASSEL. The Bn came under the command of the 5th Infy Bde (2nd Divn).	
do.	5th		The day was spent in cleaning up & improving billets.	
do	6th		Inspection of A Coy, clothing by the Comdg. Officer. The Battn bathed at the Bde Baths, DORMAGEN.	

D. D. & L., London, E.C.
(A8604) Wt. W.2771/M2-31 730,000 5/17 Sch. 33 Forms/C2118/14

Army Form C. 2118.

WAR DIARY
or
INTELLIGENCE SUMMARY.
(Erase heading not required.)

Place	Date	Hour	Summary of Events and Information	Remarks and references to Appendices
Germany	March 7th		Comdg. Officer inspection of clothing. Bn. Soccer match.	
do	8th		Comdg Officer inspection of clothing. Games.	
do	9th		Church Parade.	
do	10th		Coy training. B. Coy moved to LONGEERICH to relieve a detachment of the 2nd H.L.I. finding guards over 2nd Army ammunition dump.	
do	11th		The Battn. was inspected by the Army Commander Genl Sir H PLUMER. The Bn paraded in close column of coys. on the parade ground FUHLINGEN at 14:30 hours. The Army Commander inspected the whole of the Bn, including the transport + complimented the CmDg Officer on the general smartness + turn out of all ranks. The Battn then marched passed in column of fours.	

WAR DIARY
or
INTELLIGENCE SUMMARY.

(Erase heading not required.)

Army Form C. 2118.

Place	Date	Hour	Summary of Events and Information	Remarks and references to Appendices
[do]	March 12		N.C.O's mess R.S.M. games.	
do	13.		B. Ron C March. When the Cin-C officer, knik knyel fuhlinger - the kink & Michrisil	
do	14.		by Jaany. Victories Wahigda returned on of what did win in the after in the lecture hall, FUHLINGEN.	
do	15.		The long typer inspected legs at Platoon and by Batt. Cs mat. L.	
do	16.		Church parades.	
do	17.		The Battn. Less B. Coy moved to WORRINGEN.	
do	18.		(Training up. Improvement of Billets etc.)	
do	19.		Battn. Parade. Arct. compulsory education classes recommenced.	
do	20.		Battn. Parade (am & pm) Games C.C.	
do	21.		Battn. Ron G. March.	
do	22.		Coy parade. Lecture by Major Hillop, on German German.	
do	23.		Church Parades. Education class. (General analysis) communal	
do	24.		Coy Jaany. Father Fry Evening Lecture at the Jute factory, Beginnings of Break out & transportations were completed by destroyed owing to the fact that Payte.	
do	25.		Coy Jaany. WORRINGEN. The faeries were avealed the No. B Battn. found but I analen of finguished appliances war avealed by keeping order, removing families from house in the whole of the fire. No troops were billeted on or near the factor.	

Army Form C. 2118.

WAR DIARY
or
INTELLIGENCE SUMMARY.
(Erase heading not required.)

4.

Place	Date	Hour	Summary of Events and Information	Remarks and references to Appendices
Germany	March 26th		Coy. Training. Lecture by Rev. Hunter Boyd. Games.	
do	27th		Coy. Training. Tactical Schemes for all Officers.	
do	28th		Batt. Route March.	
do	29th		Coy. Training. Baths at Dormagen Factory. A shell loading party of 3 Officers & 150 O.R. was found at Dormagen. A/Capt D.L. MacLean, 2/Lt. C.E. Goody, 2/Lt. H.W. Shearcroft joined from the 2nd Batt.	
do	30th		Church Parade. 2/Lt. J. Wheeler joined from the 2nd Batt. Capt. C.R. Stuart, 2/Lt. G.W.S. Brown, 2/Lt. E.J. Plant joined from the 2nd Batt. K.R.R.C. via the 25th Bn. K.R.R.C. 2/Lt. H.A. Hawley left to join the 25th K.R.R.C.	
do	31st		Coy. Training. 2/Lt. H.A. Sykes & 2/Lt. H.A. Hawley left for England. Capt. M. Hamilton R.A.M.C. attd. left for England.	

V. Rader Lt.

Army Form C. 2118.

52ⁿᵈ Battn. The Rifle Brigade.

WAR DIARY
or
INTELLIGENCE SUMMARY.
(Erase heading not required.)

Instructions regarding War Diaries and Intelligence Summaries are contained in F.S. Regs., Part II. and the Staff Manual respectively. Title pages will be prepared in manuscript.

Place	Date	Hour	Summary of Events and Information	Remarks and references to Appendices
Morringen	April 1.		Company Training.	
	2.		Company Training. Capt. C.R. Stuart transferred from C. to A. Coy.	
	3.		Inspection by Brigadier General Commanding 1ˢᵗ Right Bde.	
	4.		Bathing. Lectured by Lt. Col. Seymour Bullock. Capt. C.S. Tennant R.A.M.C. joined for duty.	
	5.		Preparation for move to Konigshoven. Lieut. Everett, 2/Lt. Nove M.M., 2/Lt. Laithwaite joined for duty from 2ⁿᵈ Bn. The Rifle Bde.	
			Capt. Marshall M.C. - Capt. Barrass, Lieut. Dumpson left for demobilisation.	
			Capt. C.R. Stuart appointed O.C. A. Coy. vice Capt. Marshall M.C. (demob)	
	6.		2/Lt. G.W.S. Brown appointed Bn. Signalling Officer.	
			Church Parade. Capt. C. Tennant R.A.M.C. left.	
			Bn. moved by rail from Morringen to Konigshoven.	
Konigshoven	7.		Arranging & cleaning up. Lt. Buller, Capt. G.W. Shaw R.A.M.C. reports.	
	8.		Lt. H. Stably M.C. joined for duty from 2ⁿᵈ Bn. The Rifle Brigade.	
	9.		Inspection of C & D Coys by Commdg. Officer.	
	10.		Inspection of A & B Coys by Commdg. Officer.	
	11.		Company Training.	
	12.		Company Training. S. Sports.	
	13.		Church Parade. S. Sports.	

R. Mimi Stff
Comd 52ⁿᵈ Bn. The Rifle Brigade

52nd Battn. The Rifle Brigade

Army Form C. 2118.

WAR DIARY
or
INTELLIGENCE SUMMARY.

(Erase heading not required.)

Place	Date	Hour	Summary of Events and Information	Remarks and references to Appendices
KONIGSHOVEN	April 14.		Company Training. The Battn joins the Third Guard. (12 days).	
	15.		Inspection by Brigadier General, Commanding 3rd Lights Brigade.	
	16.		Company Training. Lecture by C.O. to Officers, M.O's & N.C.O's. Soccer Match v. 53 R.B.	
	17.		Company Training.	
	18.		Company Training. Voluntary Church Parade. Shoot. Capt. Norris C.F. reports to duty.	
	19.		Good Friday. Voluntary Church Parade. 2/Lt. A. Barnaby promoted to Lieut.	
	20.		Company Training. Inter Platoon on a side soccer competition won by 15/16 Toon.	
	21.		Church Parade. Inter Platoon B. Soccer Match.	
	22.		Holiday.	
	23.		B. Route March.	
	24.		Company Training.	
	25.		Company Training.	
	26.		Inspection of Bat. Respirators by Gas Officer. Company Training. B. Rugby Match v. 53 Rifle Bn. (Won Jan B.)	
	27.		Company Training. Games.	
	28.		Church Parade.	
	29.		Company Training. Games.	
	30.		Battn Route March. Inspection of Rifles by Armourer Sergt.	

V. Rieme Lt
Comdg. 52nd Bn. The Rifle Brigade

Army Form C. 2118.

52nd Battn. The Rifle Brigade

WAR DIARY
or
INTELLIGENCE SUMMARY.
(Erase heading not required.)

Place	Date	Hour	Summary of Events and Information	Remarks and references to Appendices
Horsweges	April 1.		Company training. Capt. B.R. Stuart. Transferred from C to A Coy.	
	2.		Company training. Capt. B. transferred from C to 1st Rifle Bn.	
	3.		Inspection by Brigadier General commanding 1st Rifle Bde.	
	4.		Bathing. Returned to Bn. Col. Symon Bullock & Capt. W.S. Tennant R.A.M.C. joined for duty	
	5.		Preparation for move to Konigshoven. M. Lieut. Ewen N.- 2/Lt Have NM-2/Lt Haw Edwards (?)	
			Joined for duty from 2nd Bn. The Rifle Bde.	
			Capt. Marshall M.C.- Capt. Burgess, Lieut Simpson left for demobilisation	
			Capt. C.R. Stuart appointed O.C. A Coy vice Capt. Marshall M.C. (class 6)	
			Capt. G.W.S. Brown appointed 2nd Bn. Adjutant Officer	
			2/Lt G.W.S. Brown appointed	
	6.		Church Parade. Capt. C. Tennant R.A.M.C. to A	
			Bn. moved by rail from Morringon to Konigshoven	
KONIGSHOVEN	7.		Arranging & cleaning up. J. Bullek. Capt. J. W. Shaw R.A.M.C. & for Co.	
	8.		Lt. H.H. Dully M.C. posted for duty from 2nd Bn. The Rifle Brigade	
	9.		Inspection of C&D Coys by Comdg Officer	
	10.		Inspection of A & B Coys by Comdg Officer	
	11.		Company Training. Sports	
	12.		Company Training. Sports	
	13.		Church Parade. Sports.	

V. Rainu Fitt
Comdg 52nd Bn. The Rifle Brigade

Army Form C. 2118.

"52" Batt. The Rifle Brigade
WAR DIARY
or
INTELLIGENCE SUMMARY.
(Erase heading not required.)

Instructions regarding War Diaries and Intelligence Summaries are contained in F. S. Regs., Part II. and the Staff Manual respectively. Title pages will be prepared in manuscript.

Place	Date	Hour	Summary of Events and Information	Remarks and references to Appendices
KÖNIGSHOVEN	Apr 14		Company Training. The Battn. joins the Advd Guard. (12/1935)	
	15.		Inspection by Brigadier General commanding 3rd Light Brigade.	
	16.		Company Training. Lecture by C.O. to officers, W.O.s & N.C.O.s. Soccer Match V. 53 R.B.	
	17.		Company Training.	
	18.		(Good Friday). Voluntary Church Parade. 2/Lt E. Batt. Norris C.F. ad/m to spec duty	
	19.		Company Training. 2/Lt A. Barnaby promoted Lieut.	
	20.		Church Parade & Games.	
	21.		Holiday. Inter Platoon 244 a side soccer competition. Won by 15/16 Platoon.	
	22.		B. Route March. B. Soccer Match.	
	23.		Company Training.	
	24.		Company Training.	
	25.		Instruction of Batt. Respirator by Gas Officer. Company Training	
	26.		Company Training. Games. Bd Ry by Match v. 53" Rifle Bde. (won for B.)	
	27.		Church Parade. Games.	
	28.		Company Training. Games.	
	29.		Battn. Route March. Inspection of Rifles by Armourer Sergt.	
	30.		Company Training.	

Riddell Lt Col
Comdg. 52nd Bn. The Rifle Brigade

52nd Batn. The Rifle Brigade

WAR DIARY or INTELLIGENCE SUMMARY.
Army Form C. 2118.

Place	Date	Hour	Summary of Events and Information	Remarks and references to Appendices
Königslouter	May 1st		Company Training. A Coys. Rifles reviewed by armourer Sergt.	
	2"		do. do. B do. do. do.	
	3		do. do. Sports.	
	4.		Church Parade	
	5.		A+B Coys. on 30 yds range. C+D Company Training.	
	6.		3rd Light Brigade inspected by H.R.H. The Duke of Connaught. The Bn. furnished to BEDBURG by bus in the morning, camped in a field for dinner, and cleared away. After the inspection the Bn. marched past H.R.H and then marched back to R. to billets.	
	7.		Company Training. Lecture to A+B Coys by M.O.	
	8.		C+D. Coys on 30 yds range. A+B Company training. Lecture by M.O. to C+D Coys	
	9.		Company Training. 8 H.R. O. Transferred to 3rd Light T.M. Battery	
	10.		Adjt. Regt. Parade. Arms and Gas Drill.	
	11.		Church Parade. Rugby match versus Tyoole Hus. Corps 9 Hours Bn. 8/Jun 6	
	12.		Company Training. Maj. Hayward (London Regt) lectured on Bilgium L.I.	
	13.		Bn. Rte to March. Lecture by M.O.	

A6945 Wt. W11422/M1160 350,000 12/16 D. D. & L. Forms/C./2118/14.

"52nd Battn. The Rifle Brigade."

WAR DIARY
or
INTELLIGENCE SUMMARY.
(Erase heading not required.)

Army Form C. 2118.

Place	Date	Hour	Summary of Events and Information	Remarks and references to Appendices
Königshoven	May 14		Company training.	
	15.		Batt. Parade under Comdg. Officer.	
	16.		Company training. Mr. J. Ramsbottom gave "Miscellaneous Recitals".	
	17.		R.S.M's Parade. Arms and Gas Drill.	
	18.		Church Parade. A v. B Coy cricket match.	
	19.		A & B boys on range. C & D boys, company training.	
	20.		Treasure Hunt.	
	21.		C & D boys 30 yds range. A & B boys company training. The final of the Bee Football Competition for the G.O.C's Cup was played at BEDBURG between 6th F.A. Field Ambulance. Result: 6th F.A. 3 goals A Coy 1 goal.	
	22.		A Coy of the Bn and 6th Field Ambulance.	
			A & B boys on range. C & D Company training 6a/12 D. Kennedy an 2/Lt H.W. Sheaves-Smith left for demobilization.	
	23.		C & D boys on range. A & B Coys company training.	
	24.		Empire Day. Holiday. Hy & Bn. donicket 1 Match.	
	25.		Church Parade. Half Bn. cricket match.	
	26.		Adjutant's Parade. Officers W.O's & Sergts under C.O. for Tactical Exercise.	

Army Form C. 2118.

52nd Battn. The Rifle Brigade.

WAR DIARY
or
INTELLIGENCE SUMMARY.
(Erase heading not required.)

Place	Date	Hour	Summary of Events and Information	Remarks and references to Appendices
KONIGSHOVEN	May 27		Bn. Route March, finishing with "Artillery formation" practice.	
	28		C. & D. Coys on range. A & B. Company Training. Lecture "Outposts" by C.O.	
	29		A & B. Coys on range. C & D coys. company training.	
	30		C & D coys range. A & B. Company Training. 3 Kr. Trans Jews to 205	
	31		Employment Day. Comdg Officers Parade. G.O.C. Light Division inspected cookhouses and canteen of the Bn.	

[signature]

for Lieut. Colonel Comdg. 52nd Bn
The Rifle Brigade

The R.B. 52nd Battn. Brigade

Army Form C. 2118.

WAR DIARY
or
INTELLIGENCE SUMMARY. JUNE 1919.

(Erase heading not required.)

Place	Date	Hour	Summary of Events and Information	Remarks and references to Appendices
Kingstown	June 1st		Church Parade.	NR
	2nd		Company Training. Tactical Scheme for Officers N.C.O's & Sergts.	NR
	3rd		Kings Birthday. Bath. Parade. Proc. A. Royal Salute was given followed by three cheers for H.M. The remainder of the day was observed as a holiday.	NR
	4th		Company Training.	NR
	5th		Company Training.	NR
	6th		Company Training. Cricket Match.	NR
	7th		Lewis Gun Teams large twelve Coy. Bn. Cricket match.	NR
	8th		Church Parade. Cricket Match (with company)	NR
	9th		Bn Athletic Meeting. In the presence of Major General Sir R.D. Whigham K.C.B. K.C.M.G. D.S.O. Challenge Cup won by H Company. Officers Riding School started.	NR
	10th		Company Training. Mule Race for Transport Personnel.	NR
	11th		Company Training.	NR
	12th		Company Training. Lewis Gun Teams on Range.	Review for NR
	13th		Bn Route March.	NR

Army Form C. 2118.

The Rifle Bde 52nd Bn.

WAR DIARY
or
INTELLIGENCE SUMMARY

(Erase heading not required.)

JUNE 1919

Instructions regarding War Diaries and Intelligence Summaries are contained in F. S. Regs., Part II. and the Staff Manual respectively. Title pages will be prepared in manuscript.

Place	Date	Hour	Summary of Events and Information	Remarks and references to Appendices
	JUNE			
Konigshoven	14		Company Training. Cricket Match.	NR
	15		Church Parades.	NR
	16		Company Training	NR
	17		Bn received orders to move to Cologne	NR
Line of March	18		The Bn moved by march route to STOMMELN. (13 miles)	NR
"	19		The march was continued to MUNGERSDORF. (8½ miles) Billeting accommodation poor.	NR
Mungersdorf	20		The day was spent at Mungersdorf	NR
Line of March	21		The Bn marched from Mungersdorf to Wilks in the Bergernather Strasse,	NR
July Cologne			Cologne, July. The Comdg Officer, Adjt & Officer of D Coy reconnoitred the bridges (Hohenzollern, Mülheim & Suod), from 16 to King Thies guards every from the London S Divn.	
	22		Church Parade	NR
	23		Company Training was continued. Tactical Scheme for Officers under C.O.	NR
	24		Tactical Scheme. Defence of a locality, (the old fortification of Cologne was used).	NR
	25		Company Training	NR
	26		Company Training	NR

A Raim Lt.

The Rifle 52nd Battn. Rifle Brigade

Army Form C. 2118.

WAR DIARY
or
INTELLIGENCE SUMMARY. JUNE 1919.

(Erase heading not required.)

Place	Date	Hour	Summary of Events and Information	Remarks and references to Appendices
July-Cologne	JUNE 27th		Bn. Route March.	VR
	28th		Company Training	VR
	29th		Church Parade. Orders received for Bn. to return to old billets.	VR
	30.		The Bn. moved by march route to STOMMELN. (12 miles) marching very good	VR

Reiner Lt. Col.
Comdg. 52" Battn. The Rifle Brigade

WAR DIARY or INTELLIGENCE SUMMARY.

Army Form C. 2118.

(Erase heading not required.)

Place	Date	Hour	Summary of Events and Information	Remarks and references to Appendices
Kirkpatrick	July 1		Tactical Scheme - Officers & Sgts under Commanding Officer - Games	NR
	2		Coy Training - Interior Economy & Kit Inspection - Sports	NR
	3		Coys on Range - Education	NR
	4		Coy Training - Lecture by Lt Col Lt. Tyke M.S.V.R. "Life and occupations in the Malay States" G#4 no educational instructor	NR - 2 NCOs reported for NR
	5		Coy Training - Games	NR
	6		Church Parade - Cricket 3-2 v 5 Rfl Bde V 157 7 Fuls Coy T.E.	NR NR
	7		Packing and cleaning up and arranging move to H.L.DEN.	NR
	8		[illegible] Labour	NR
HILDEN	9/10		Battalion moved to HILDEN - Coys at HOLTHAUSEN and DAMMSTE & POSTS. Coy Training - Commanding Officers inspects [illegible] - Sports	NR NR
	11		Coy Training - Rifle and Inspection - Games	NR
	12		Coy Training - Games	NR
	13		Church Parade - Cricket	NR
	14		Coy Training - Games	NR
	15		Battalion Route March - Return from [illegible] War Read out to Troops	NR

[signatures] NR Rfl Rfl Lt.

WAR DIARY
or
INTELLIGENCE SUMMARY.
(Erase heading not required.)

Army Form C. 2118.

Place	Date	Hour	Summary of Events and Information	Remarks and references to Appendices
HILDEN	July 16		Coy Training - Games - 6 Rfn transferred to 6th Field Ambulance	NR
	17		Coy Training - Games - 23 Rfn " " 12th Lancers	NR
	18		Coy Training - Coy on range - Games	NR
	19		Coy Training - Billets inspected by Commanding	NR
	20		Church Parade - Cricket	NR
	21		Coy Training - Sports	NR
	22		Battalion Route March	NR
	23		Holiday - Peace Celebration	NR
	24		Coy Training - Games	NR
	25		Coy Training - 9.12 Rfn Re Enlisted and 5 sent on furlough	NR
	26		Coy Training - Lecture by RSM - Games	NR
	27		Church Parade - Cricket	NR
	28		Coy Parade - Games	NR
	29		Battalion Route March	NR
	30		Coy Training - Tactical Scheme in Wood Fighting -	NR
	31		Coy Training - Lecture on War Savings -	NR

N Ricou Lt/Col R Rfn
Col 5th Bn Rfn Bde

52nd Battn.
The Rifle Brigade

WAR DIARY
or
INTELLIGENCE SUMMARY
(Erase heading not required.)

Army Form C. 2118.

ORDERLY ROOM -2 SEP 1919 52nd

Place	Date	Hour	Summary of Events and Information	Remarks and references to Appendices
Aldon	August 1		Company Training. Lecture "Cause of the Rise + Fall of Nations by Prof W. MacDougall	AR
	2		Company Training	AR
	3		Church Parades	AR
	4		Bank Holiday Sports	AR
	5		Company Training. Games. 2 Officers + 43 OR. went for a Rhine Trip.	AR
	6		Company Training. The Bn. was equipped with webbing equipment + the	AR
			leather equipment was returned to Ordnance.	AR
	7		Company Training	AR
	8		Divnl Commander visited the Bn. Musketry Instruction	AR
	9		Company Training	AR
	10		Church Parades. Bucket Match. C.O. voiced the funnels.	AR
	11		Company Training	AR
	12		"A" Company commenced firing General Musketry Course.	AR
	13		A Coy. firing G.M.C. B. Coy. Coy. Training C+D Outpost Line	AR
	14		A + B Coys. G.M.C.	AR
	15		do do	AR

V. Rieven Lt.

52nd Battn
The Rifle Brigade.

WAR DIARY
or
INTELLIGENCE SUMMARY.

Army Form C. 2118.

Place	Date	Hour	Summary of Events and Information	Remarks and references to Appendices
Hilden	August 16		A & B. Companies firing G.M.C. C & D. Coys. Outpost Line	IR
	17		A. Company finished firing G.M.C. do.	IR
	18		B.Company firing G.M.C. A. Coy cleaning up.	IR
	19		A. Company relieved C. Company in the Outpost Line. B. Company continues firing the G.M.C.	IR
	20		B. Company firing G.M.C. C. Company organising Athletics	IR
	21		B. Company firing. A Brigade "Eliminating Contest" was held in the afternoon in connection with the Army Athletic Championships. The Bn. won the cup for Athletic Events	IR IR
	22		C. Company commenced firing G.M.C. Brigade Eliminating Contest continued. The Bn. won the Cross Country Run Cup.	IR
	23		C. Company firing G.M.C.	IR
	24		B.Company relieved D. Company in the outpost line. C. Company continued firing the G.M.C.	IR
	25		Regimental Birthday Holiday. A short meeting was held by the Officers Battalion of the Regiment in the Brigade.	IR

V. Riddell Lt Col

Army Form C. 2118.

52nd Batn.
The Rifle Brigade

WAR DIARY
or
INTELLIGENCE SUMMARY.
(Erase heading not required.)

Instructions regarding War Diaries and Intelligence Summaries are contained in F. S. Regs., Part II. and the Staff Manual respectively. Title pages will be prepared in manuscript.

Place	Date	Hour	Summary of Events and Information	Remarks and references to Appendices
Hildin	August 26		C. Company continued firing G.M.C. D. Company commenced firing G.M.C.	AR
	27		C & D Company continued firing the G.M.C.	AR
	28		C. Company finished and D. Company continued firing the G.M.C.	AR
	29		D. Company continued firing G.M.C. C. Company company training	AR
	30		C. Company training. D. Company G.M.C.	AR
	31		Church Parade. D. Company finished firing G.M.C.	AR

W Reeve Lt. Colonel.
Comdg. 52nd Battalion.
The Rifle Brigade.

August 31st 1919.

The Rifle Brigade. 52nd Battalion.

WAR DIARY or INTELLIGENCE SUMMARY.
(Erase heading not required.)

Army Form C. 2118.

Place	Date	Hour	Summary of Events and Information	Remarks and references to Appendices
Guisnes Hilsow	September 1st		Company training	TW
"	2nd		R.S.M's Parade. Company Training. 12 prisoners taken at Damery big post and four at Holthausen for attempting B.G.C. visited outpost companies.	TW
"	3rd		Company Training. 4 prisoners taken by outpost companies for attempting to bribe and two captured in the wire near Hammely endeavouring to cross into occupied territory without passes.	TW
"	4th		Tactical Exercise for the two companies billeted in Hilsow. Divisional Sports held in the afternoon. 5 prisoners taken at Holthausen.	TW
"	5th		Company Training. Divisional Cross Country run.	TW
"	6th		Inspection of the two companies billeted in Hilsow by the Brigade Officer.	TW
"	7th		Church Parade. Bn cricket match.	TW
"	8th		The two companies billeted in Hilsow were inspected by the G.O.C. Light Division. C company was given a tactical exercise to carry out and D Coy was inspected at Company Drill.	TW
"	9th		C and D Companies relieved A and B Companies in the Outpost line.	TW
"	10th		Company Training. 2 Prisoners taken during the day	TW

52nd Battalion.
The Rifle Brigade

Army Form C. 2118.

WAR DIARY
or
INTELLIGENCE SUMMARY.
(Erase heading not required.)

Instructions regarding War Diaries and Intelligence Summaries are contained in F. S. Regs, Part II. and the Staff Manual respectively. Title pages will be prepared in manuscript.

Place	Date	Hour	Summary of Events and Information	Remarks and references to Appendices
Germany Hilden	Sept 10th		A and B Companies inspected by the Brig. Officer.	TW
"	11th		Route March for Bn. Two companies on Outpost Duties.	TW
"	12th		R.S.M's Parade. Officers and Senior N.C.O's, Tactical exercise under the C.O.	TW
"	13th		Church Parades. 2 Prisoners taken for attempting to escape	TW
"	14th		Company Training. Gas Drill under Brigade Gas N.C.O.	TW
"	15th		A and B Companies relieved by C & D Companies in the Outpost Line.	TW
"	16th		Company Training. 5 Prisoners taken at Dammstep Post.	TW
"	17th		R.S.M's Parade. Tactical Exercise for Officers, Warrant and N.C.Os under C.O.	TW
"	18th		Tactical Exercise for the two companies billeted in Hilden Dif	TW
"	19th		Prisoners taken at Dammstep.	TW
"	20th		Inspection of two companies by Brig. Officer. One prisoner taken and one German wounded at Friedrichsposs attempting to enter occupied territory through the wire. 7 prisoners taken at Holthausen	TW TW
"	21st		Church Parades.	TW
"	22nd		Casuals Parades for musketry. G.O.C. Light Division visited Outpost Line.	TW
"	23rd		Casuals commenced firing the G.M.E. several prisoners taken during the day.	TW

Army Form C. 2118.

The Rifle Brigade. 52nd Battalion.

WAR DIARY
or
INTELLIGENCE SUMMARY.
(Erase heading not required.)

Instructions regarding War Diaries and Intelligence Summaries are contained in F. S. Regs., Part II. and the Staff Manual respectively. Title pages will be prepared in manuscript.

Place	Date	Hour	Summary of Events and Information	Remarks and references to Appendices
Germany Hilden	September 24th		The Casuals continued firing the G.M.G. Ten Gunners selected during the day by outposts.	TW
"	25th		Casuals continued firing. 13 Prisoners taken at Damastig Post.	TW
"	26th		Casuals finished firing the G.M.G. 3 Prisoners taken for attempted robbery.	TW
"	27th		The Lewis Gunner commenced firing their annual course. Seven Prisoners taken.	TW
"	28th		Lewis Gunners continued firing.	TW
"	29th		The Lewis Gunners finished firing their annual course. Seven Prisoners taken at Holthausen.	TW
"	30th		Company Training. Tents evacuated at Wamsleg and men moved into billets.	TW

TW———
Major.
Commanding 52nd Battalion
The Rifle Brigade

Instructions regarding War Diaries and Intelligence Summaries are contained in F.S. Regs., Part II. and the Staff Manual respectively. Title pages will be prepared in manuscript.

Duplicate copy has been rendered to O/c Rifle Records Manchester

Army Form C. 2118.

WAR DIARY
or
INTELLIGENCE SUMMARY.
(Erase heading not required.)

Place	Date	Hour	Summary of Events and Information	Remarks and references to Appendices
HILDEN	Oct. 1st		Company Training. Tactical scheme for Offrs. W.Os, & N.C.Os, under the C.O.	
do	2nd	0930	Tactical exercise. Football and Games.	
do	3rd		Company Training. Rate of exchange = 120 Mks to £1 sterling.	
do	4th		Company Training and games in the afternoon	
do	5th		Church Parades. Football.	
do	6th		Company Training. Games in the afternoon.	
do	7th		Commanding Officer's Inspection. Football	
do	8th		Company Training.	
do	9th		Commanding Officer's Inspection of the Battalion and Transport. Games.	
do	10th		Company Training - Rugby Football in the afternoon at Benrath.	
do	11th		Musketry Results published. Company Training. 6 Offrs & 132 O.Rs to Cologne on detachment duty	
do	12th		Church Parades - Alteration in from summer to winter time.	
do	13th		Company Training & Games.	
do	14th		Fatigue party taking beds to Opladen. Lieut.Col. E.P.A. Riddell, CMG., DSO., to England.	
do	15th		Packing up for move to Opladen.	
do	16th		Move to Opladen postponed indefinitely. Interior Economy.	

A6945 Wt. W14422/M180 350,000 12/16 D.D. & L. Forms/C/2118/14.

Army Form C. 2118.

WAR DIARY
or
INTELLIGENCE-SUMMARY.
(Erase heading not required.)

Instructions regarding War Diaries and Intelligence Summaries are contained in F. S. Regs., Part II. and the Staff Manual respectively. Title pages will be prepared in manuscript.

Place	Date	Hour	Summary of Events and Information	Remarks and references to Appendices
HILDEN	17th		Alteration in rate of exchange, i.e. 109&10Mks= £1 Sterling.	
do	18th		Company Training - 18 men to demobilization. Football.	
do	19th		Church Parade in the Outpost Line. Football and games in the afternoon.	
do	20th		Company Training - Football.	
do	21st		Company Training - Games and Football - Rugby Practice. Move to Benrath	
BENRATH	22nd		11 Officers and 344 O.Rs on strength from 53rd Bn. The Rifle Brigade.	
do	23rd		Company Training - Interior Economy - Signallers parade under Signalling Officer daily.	
do	24th		Commanding Officer's Inspection of "A" & "D" Companies. Football.	
do	25th		Company Training. Games and Football in the afternoon.	
do	26th		Church parades in Protestant Church. Promulgation of F.G.C.M.	
do	27th		Company Training. Games.	
do	28th		C.O.-s Lecture to Officers on Military Law. Company Parades and Football.	
do	29th		Company Parades. Rugby Football Match -v1½ 20th Bn. K.R.R.C. at Solingen.	
do	30th		Company Training - R.S.M's parade. Sergeants' Mess Meeting - Football.	
do	31st		Company Training - Rugby Football match against 12th Royal Irish Rifles in the afternoon	

Major Commanding 52nd Battn THE RIFLE BRIGADE

www.ingramcontent.com/pod-product-compliance
Lightning Source LLC
Chambersburg PA
CBHW081504160426
43193CB00014B/2586